DR NORMAN WATSON was a journalist with *The Courier* in Dundee for 25 years and wrote more than 5,000 news features for the paper. He remains a *Courier* columnist and is now publishing giant DC Thomson's first-ever company historian.

An award-winning author, his books include the best-selling *Dundee: A Short History* (2006), *The Biography of William McGonagall* (2010) and the internationally-acclaimed *Dundee Dicshunury* (2012).

As an historian he has co-curated major exhibitions in Dundee, London and Edinburgh and in 2006 was invited to open the Scottish Parliament's first-ever public exhibition.

'Eh hud meh ehe on a peh'

The best of the best of those
mouthwatering Dundee sayings

NORMAN WATSON

Illustrations by
BOB DEWAR

Luath Press Limited

EDINBURGH

www.luath.co.uk

First published 2016
Reprinted 2017
Reprinted 2018
Reprinted 2019

ISBN: 978-1-910745-83-0

The paper used in this book is recyclable. It is made from
low chlorine pulps produced in a low energy, low emissions manner
from renewable forests.

Printed and bound by
Bell & Bain Ltd., Glasgow

Typeset in Quadraat and MetaPlus
by 3btype.com

The author's right to be identified as author of this work under the
Copyright, Designs and Patents Act 1988 has been asserted.

© Norman Watson 2016

Contents

Introduction

Dundonians have a defining, distinctive way of expressing themselves and communicating feelings. The ancient city's characteristic accent can be heard in any Lochee bar or Hilltoon playground, or on any bus – where Dundee grannies have extraordinary 'Eh?' 'Eh!' nodding conversations. And to the trained ear they make perfect sense!

Great Dundonesian favourites have passed into folklore – such as 'Twa plehn bridies an' an ingin ane 'n' a'; or 'Eh'll hae a peh' or the ubiquitous and unique parting phrase, 'See yi ehfter'.

The 'sayings' in this work delve into this peh eatin' democracy to cover appearance, clothes, drink, expressions, family life, health, human behaviour, insults, love, money and, of course, Dundonian philosophy!

Much credit for the survival of Dundonese is due to the unofficial ambassador of local dialect David Phillips, whose books in the 1960s and 1970s ensured words, phrases and grammatical features wiz kept alehve. The baton passed to Mick McCluskey in the 1990s and then to my own *Dundee Dicshunury* of 2011. To those who helped with this new collection, including Kevin Breen of Waterstone's Dundee, sincere thanks are due.

Hopefully, these sayings will resonate with Dundonians and their kin the world over.

With nae offence meant t'naebody, enjoy!

NUMPTAY RD

Insults

Awa 'n' keech.

No thanks.

Ut'er nu'er.

A headbanger.

S'allota baloney!

You're talking rubbish.

Goota m'sicht.

Perhaps you would consider going away?

M'ere you!

Do you want a bit?

Whut's yir face trippin' ye fur now?

Is something wrong?

See ane aff ye, ye wee crab.

Can I have one, please?

Yer as yaiseless as a pile of snottirz.

I don't think you've got the hang of this.

That nu'er needs the jile.

That idiot might be better behind bars.

Eez puir aff his heid.

That chap is sadly lacking in
worldly direction.

She huza nerse like m'auhld ermchair.

She's put on the pounds, that one.

Hezza cumplete numptay.

He isn't the full shilling.

Dinna gie's yir pa'er.

I think your verbose is distasteful.

Bollocks, yi big haivir.

I disagree.

The ahld gehzir's dottl'd.

The elderly chap's a bit disorientated.

Cheeky wee get.

Less of your lip, sonny.

Yir heid's the sehze o' the Lah.

Don't be so arrogant.

She's gotta puss like a burglar's dug.

She's no beauty.

His coupon wid mak Concorde fleh backwards.

He's no beauty himself.

'EH HUD ME EHE ON A PEH'

FINTRY

Dundeh Vehlence

Wud ye ublehj beh repeatin' that, pal?

Pardon?

Pit up yer dukes.

Please raise your hands for a square go.

Eh'll gie ye sumhin ti greet aboot.

Stop crying, or else!

'EH HUD ME EHE ON A PEH'

Eh'll tak meh hand aff yir jah!

Don't think I wouldn't thump you.

Thir's a guid belt inthi gub on the weh.

Prepare to be struck, sir.

Nae ixcuse fir haein' a swipe ut iz.

It had nothing to do with me.

Let behgones be behgones? Nae chans.

You haven't heard the last of this.

Meh Dad's bigger nur baith o' wiz.

I'm not afraid of you.

Gie the brat a banjoein'.

He deserves a slap.

'EH HUD ME EHE ON A PEH'

Whuturyi inseenuatin'?

Come again?

'Mere a meenit an' Eh'll brak yer jah!

Want some?

Eh'll gie ye sumthin' tae creh fur.

Belt up!

Mince kin minimehse a keeker.

That black eye needs attention.

M'affy sorry.

Please accept my apology.

Comings and Goings

Y'up?

Are you up yet?

Eh, m'up.

Yes, I'm up.

'EH HUD ME EHE ON A PEH'

Yewah?

Are you leaving?

Eh, m'wah.

Yes, I'm off.

Migit'in oot?

Can I go out?

Kinni?

Can I?

How kinnino?

Why not?

M'wah oot.

See you after.

Yoot?

Are you out?

Ehfternuin.

Good afternoon.

Eh'll hae tae shoot.

Sorry, got to go.

Whururye fae?

Where are you from?

Wharalla git a bus fae?

Do you know where the bus-stop is?

Eh'm awa' furra dander.

I'm going out for a dander.

Mupfuriz.

Would you like to call on me?

See yi ehfter.

Eponymous Dundee parting greeting,
and 'never see you later.'

Wise Words

If at furst ye dinae succeed, treh, treh agehn.

Never give up.

In furra penny, in furra poond.

If you're going to take a risk it might as well be a big one.

Yir a lang time deid.

Lighten up. Enjoy life while you can.

'EH HUD ME EHE ON A PEH'

Itz nae use crehin' ovir spult mulk.

There's no use moaning about things.

Ivry dug huz its dey.

Everyone will have good fortune
at some point.

Twa heids ur beh'ir thin wan.

Teamworking is the best option.

A's weel that ends weel.

Meaning that everything's ended well.

It isnae ovir till it's ovir.

It isn't finished yet.

Proof o' the puddin's in the aitin' o' it.

You can only judge the quality of something
after you have tried it.

Yi cannae hiv yir cake an' ait it.

You can't simultaneously enjoy two desirable
but incompatible alternatives.

Itza a nill wind that blaws
naebody ony guid.

It's a calamity, but someone will benefit from it.

A pictcher is wurth a thoosant wurds.

A photograph can tell a story better than words.

Behint ivry great man stauns a strong wummin.

Look behind you.

Dinae blah yir own trumpeet.

Avoid boasting about your achievements.

Oot o' sicht, oot o' mind.

People or things are quickly forgotten.

Bu'er widna melt in hiz mooth.

He is the picture of innocence.

Dinae beat aboot the bush.

Say what you mean.

Fowir ehes ur behr'n twa.

Four eyes are better than two.

Nae news is guid news.

Not hearing news suggests nothing is wrong.

Oot o' the frehin' pan an' intae the fehre.

From one spot of bother to another.

It taks twa tae tango.

It'll take both of us to make this work.

Weather

Brah day, izit?

Isn't it a lovely?

Wur bidin' in – it's lashin'.

You go out if you want to.

It's blahy 'n' snahy.

It's a tad wintry.

'EH HUD ME EHE ON A PEH'

S'roastin' iy?

Isn't it hot today?

S'affy cahld.

Bit chilly.

The sna's cut aff the ilectric.

We've had a black out.

Eh tellt ye it wiz cahld.

It's f-f-f-freezing.

Wahrum here, iy?

Don't you think it's hot in here?

A brah day fur pittin' oot the washin' on the greenie poles an' puhllashees.

Wash day.

The pi'er-pa'er o' rehndraps.

That's the rain on.

Familiar Questions

Ur ye, ur urn't ye?

Well, are you or aren't you?

How's yersel'?

How are you?

Whuttiye wahntin', a barra choclit?

Think you're Archie?

Mahrvluss, intit?

Isn't that good?

Jino ken?

Don't you know?

Zis no' affy?

Isn't it awful?

Ixquisit, izit?

Isn't it nice?

Eh, izit?

Yes, isn't it?

Ummat wut!

Am I really?

J'ken whit?

Do you know what?

Whut wuz whut an' wha wuz wha?

What was that all about?

Oh, meh, whuttli dae?

Oh my, what am I to do?

Whutter-yi up ti?

What's going on?

Whuttli dae a' dey?

I'm bored.

Eh, Eh wid, wid Eh?

Yes, I would, wouldn't I?

'Ji mean?

Could you repeat that, please?

May Eh intrajooce masel?

Hello.

Domestic bliss

Oh, meh, whit a bonnie teh.

My, you look smart today.

Ca canny wi' the bu'er.

Leave some butter for me.

The teapot's getting' laldy.

A woman's word is never done.

'EH HUD ME EHE ON A PEH'

Up tae the knees in can'le grease.

We're up to our knees in candle grease
– one-time Dundee playground chant.

Gie yer tongue a holiday.

Can't you stop talking for a minute?

Yiv ehes like sahcers... spile yersel'.

Shop till you drop.

Nacherly, the mair ye gie weemin, the mair they wahnt.

Husband with a death wish.

It's thay PPEh cahld callers on the phoan.

It's another personal protection insurance nuisance call.

Smell meh ermpits... that ehfter-shave is cool.

Have a whiff of that!

Eh got knocked back at the Palais.

No click for me.

Seterdays begin wi' a lang leh.

Breakfast can wait.

Yir jecket's on a shoogly nail.

You are on your final warning.

Eh nearly fell awa' when she telt iz the price.

The credit card's taken a hit.

Wir doon on wir uppers.

Life could be better.

If yi fa' and break yir leg, dinae cum runnin' tae me!

Don't say I didn't tell you.

Eez aye been a ke'ul biler.

He always stays at home to look after the bairns.

Yir rovies are reekin'.

Your slippers are minging.

That toorie's jist affy.

Your bonnet is a tad loud.

Ginfur a Tuhlay on yir weh hame.

Could you get an evening paper, please?

Eh'm awa furra Tuhlay.

Just popping out for the paper.

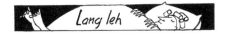

Joozhae any Tuhlays stull?

Any evening papers left?

Eh'll tak-a-Tuhlay.

I'll have a newspaper please.

J'geta Tuhlay?

Did you get a paper?

Eh'm no' an udherint o' merridge, but Eh could treh it.

In for a penny...

Retehr at suxty-fehve?
'Saffay int'restin' ehdea.

I can't afford to retire.

Whut 'n eejit.
Yir glesses are on yir heid!

Where have you not looked for your spectacles?

Oh eh, weemin drehvers.

Asking for trouble!

The neeburs ur daein' a fleh-beh-nichter.

Mr and Mrs Excheenge are doing a moonlight flit.

Eez ahl'fashint an' oot o' touch.

Dad!

Mither's furgot hur fahlsers.

Anyone seen Mum's teeth?

Wi'e eh-lids like sahcers, mauhve eh-shadie diz it fur me.

Colour blind.

Yir shaes ur in the lohbee.

Your shoes are where you left them.

Dundee life

Dighty disnae rhyme with Blighty!

Ellacution lesson, Dundee-style.

When in Dundeh,
dae as the Dundonians dae.

Always act like you are a local.

Brah.

I'm fine, thanks.

Uma wrang or uma right?

Am I wrong or am I right?

Yool git yir heid in yir hauns t'play wi'.

That's your final warning.

So?

I couldn't care less.

Ullawa furra messages.

I'm off for the shopping.

The treezur hingin' wi' aippuls.

There's a fine crop of apples this year.

Eh'm fair fed up o' yir haverin'.

Would you mind being quiet?

'EH HUD ME EHE ON A PEH'

Eh, Eh huv ehdraps in ma eh.

Yes, I've got drops in my eye.

Fansay a freh-up?

Would you like to come over for supper?

Yir'on.

Yes, please.

Itza struggle tae the Stoabbie.

It's all uphill to Stobswell.

Fulm's keech.

This film isn't very good.

Oh meh Goad!

OMG!

Rest ashaired, Eh'm echteen.

Yes, I'm old enough to drink.

Tell wiz sumhin' new.

Not that story again.

Yir like a nahld record.

Not that story again.

Yir a cahld tattie.

You're always cold.

The pair sowel's been brehnwashed.

He's besotted with it.

Eh did it meh wey.

I did my own thing.

Whuddiyi mean?

Pardon?

Meh feet ur lettin' in.

There's a hole in my wellies.

Oh ehe, he's minted.

He's made of money.

Keep the heid!

Calm down.

Gie wiz a sang.

Give us a song.

Lahrinjettis? Nattata.
Eh yaseyully sing like this.

No, this is how I normally sound.

Crehsis at the Krehmay: he's no' deid.

The Crematorium has a problem.

He jist woke up deid.

He died in his sleep.

We work our socks off for peanuts.

From Mary Brooksbank's 'Jute Mill Song.'

Whitta fleg tae gie iz.

Goodness, you surprised me.

Eh'm doon tae ma last hunerthousan' an' twa yachts.

Times are hard.

Huz the bummer blown?
Nah, it hasnae went yet.

It's not clocking off time yet.

Eh'm ovirjoo at the lehbray.

These books are due for return.

Pleh'ay.

Back stairwell feachir o' Dundeh architectchir.

Puhllashees made oot o' pleh-wid for pittin' the wahshin' oot.

Kitchen essentials.

Wha selt the gairden polie?

Anyone seen the washing line?

'Closie'.

The stairwell in a block of flats.

Circul.

Any Dundee roundabout apart from the Swallow.

Anither jeit muhll awa.

There goes another factory.

La and lah.

The La huhll and the lah in the coort.

Eh'm hingin' claes
on the claespole in the coortyaird
ahint the closie.

I'm putting out the washing in the area
behind my house.

Um no entehrely shair whaur
Discov'ry P'int iz.

Sorry, I am not a local.

Erza Ehrt Collij xeebit at D o' Jeh.

The art college has an exhibition.

Eh'm awa' tae The Ferry fir a sweem.

I am going to Broughty beach for a dook.

Up the Hackie an' doon the Blackie.

I recommend the Hawkhill,
returning via Blackness Road.

Whar's the V & Eh fae here?

How do I find the Victoria and Albert Museum?

Onythin' furthi bonie?

Any spare wood for our fireworks display?

Ye'll git sent t'the Mars.

Pacifying influence on generations of Dundee boys.

Thurza cehclist wheechin' past the Eagle Jeit Muhll.

Pedal power on Victoria Road.

Booze

Takniz furra swahlay?

Fancy a drink?

Eh'm awa' fir a swahlay.

I'm popping out for a wee refreshment.

He's iways grippit.

You'll not get a drink out of him.

Eh'm uccasionally blooter'd.

I don't mind the odd tipple or two.

'M'awa tae Mennie's.

I'm off up the Perthie for a drink.

Huv yi hud a sesh wi' Tam?

Have you been out with Thomas?

Itza naffy cerry on gettin' cheenge furra cerry-out.

It's a hassle to find the correct change to pay for our refreshments.

Boab's hud a guid buckit.

Bob's overreached himself.

Baith the twa o' uz wur flung oot backarties.

The pub chucked us out.

Ghonna staun yir haun?

Would it be your round?

Wha's roond izit ehnyweh?

Surely not my turn again?

Eh'm well wellied.

I've had a few.

Eh'm no' entehrely sober.

Perhaps I'm a little tipsy.

Fur wan affy meenit Eh thocht Eh wiz deid!

For one awful minute I thought
I wouldn't wake up.

KEN THIS

Food

**Geez a plehn ane,
an' an ingin ane 'n' a'.**

One of your delicious bridies, please,
and an onion one as well.

Eh, Eh ait it a'.

Yes, I have finished eating.

Zat no' some sez o' traikle peece?

Look at the size of that sandwich.

Eh'm no' haff stehrvin.

I'm feeling rather peckish.

'Mupfir yir tea.'

Why don't you come up for some supper?

Steik pehnpeez ur bogin.

A pie supper and peas isn't the healthy option.

Beh wan, get twa free quahrter-poonders.

Going cheap.

The best biyl't eggs biyl grahjilly.

Three minutes should do.

Wha ait Eck's East'regg?

Has someone been at Alexander's egg?

Fling iz a norange.

Could you pass me an orange, please?

Gie's a buttiyer buttie.

You'll not be needing all of that, will you?

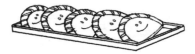

Kin Eh hae a buscuit?

May I have a biscuit?

Kinni, Mum, kinni?

Can I, Mum?

Kinnino, Mum?

Can't I, Mum?

Yaise yir loaf an' ait halemeal breid.

Be sensible – eat wholemeal bread.

He wudna ken a naippul fae a ploom.

He's more of a pie man.

Jeckit tatties huv appeal.

Baked potato for me, please.

Ileevinses.

Tea break.

'Mon, Eh'll beh yir denner.

My treat today.

Eh've jist ait an aippul.

Just had one of my five-a-day.

Deid fleh peh and a la'eh.

I'll try the fruit slice with coffee, please.

Dinae skell the sahce.

Mind the ketchup.

Thurza dumplin' inthi mehcrowave.

Your tea's on.

Wir at wur denner.

Sorry, I can't come out.

Wir ha'en oor tea.

Sorry, I can't come out.

A peh's a peh fur a' that,
ispaishully in Dundeh

Geez twa peh suppers an' a singul peh.

Pie and chips twice, please, and a single pie.

Eh hud meh ehe on a peh.

First pick to me.

Pehnpeez.

A local delicacy in the Deep Sea.

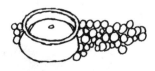

Pehzn beans.

Ditto.

It's a' peh in the skeh.

You're talking rubbish.

Waste nut, wahnt nut...
Eh'll hae a nixtra peh.

No point in wasting good food.

Nae pehs? Whut a crehsis!

Sorry, we're sold out!

Pehs ur fuhll o' mince.

The ingredients of your pie are undoubtedly mince.

Eh'll hae um'teen pehs.

Usual lunch, please.

Beh, beh, peh.

Och, I've dropped my lunch.

Dundee iza a peh-eatin' democracy.

Dundee is a pie-eating meatropolis.

'EH HUD ME EHE ON A PEH'

Gie wiz a peh furwir tea.

I'll have a pie, please.

Veejitubuls ur bogin.

I'll have a pie, please.

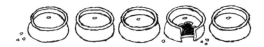

Goad, Eh've ait some pehs in meh time!

Goodness, I've eaten some pies in my time!

Sadie seghs ovir her sehze then haes twa pehs.

Liposuction awaits Sadie.

The pehs ur mince at the Chinese chipper.

Stick to what you like.

HAIVIR AVE

Medical emergencies

Eh hae a fleh in meh eh.

Something's got into my eye.

The bairnz affy no' weel.

My child is seriously off-colour today.

Eh'v a dreepie-nohsed cahld.

I've got a cold.

That biyul's mingin'.

That spot requires attention.

Meh o' meh, Eh've smudged meh lipstick.

Oh my, I've smudged my lipstick.

Eh'm awa tae be seek.

Stand back, I don't feel well.

Asp'reen's guid fur heidaches.

Use aspirin for sore heads.

Eh'm no' affy weel.

I don't feel too well.

Eh'm affy no weel.

I really don't feel very well.

Phoaniz a nambyullins!

I need medical assistance.

Pass meh ahntybehotics.

Can I have my pills, please.

M'mehgraine's nippin' ma heid.

My brain hurts.

Huv ye trehed frehd mince fur hertburn?

Fried mince might help your chest pain.

'EH HUD ME EHE ON A PEH'

Money

Beh, beh, beh...

Spend, spend, spend...

Eh'm needin' a tap till Eh get meh broo money.

Can you lend me some money until my unemployment cheque comes?

Slup iz a quid.

Can you lend me £1?

Tam, geeza lehn o' a fehvir aff yi.

Tom, would it be possible to borrow £5 from you?

Gie's a luft tae the sohshull.

Can you assist me to get to the Labour Exchange?

Twa munce tae pey dey.

Two months until the salary is paid in.

Uf coorse, a wee joab'll no' herm ye. Treh it.

Find work, you lazy git.

Eh'm iy skint, gie's a tap.

I'm a bit low on funds. Can you help?

'kettle biler'.

a term used for an unemployed man.

FINTRY

Love

She's palay wi' a'bdee.

Not the sort of girl your mother would like.

She duznae dae it furriz.

She's got a face like a bag of spanners.

She's nae chicken, that ane.

She's as old as Didh'pe Castle.

Meh bidie-in's buggert aff.

Left in the lurch.

Eh'm bissotit wi' a stottir.

I really like her.

Sehzizit? Meh!

Hmm, aren't you a big boy?

Urwi goin' oot thegither, or ur'nt we?

Are we an item?

Meh mithir-in-lah could utilehse a straightjeckit.

Bless the old girl's heart.

Dinae gie iz a minter.

Don't embarrass me.

She's the aippul o' meh eh.

There's no one else for me.

She's a'riddy spoken fur.

Just my luck!

Sadie's no haff a sexy sehrin.

Sadie does it for me.

Thir swahrmin' like flehs over Sadie.

There's no flies on Sadie.

Tak a skek at hur!

Wow, isn't she a cracker?

She's hardly a shrinkin' veholit.

She's been around a bit.

She asked iz hame.

Luck's in!

Sport and Leisure

'Znarab.

A Dundee United supporter.

Eh'm a Dee till Eh deh.

Quite keen on Dundee FC.

Wha's gaenti the Seedlies?

Anyone fancy a hike?

Y'affa yat? Which yat y'aff?

Did you arrive in Broughty Ferry by boat?
Which one?

Eh'm gehm fur Eh speh.

Would anyone like to play I spy?

Capsehzed in the Swahnnie Pahns – aband'n shup!

Boys will be boys.

Jeckets aff.

Kick-off.

Eh've t'gae hame furmi tea.

Full time.

'Fitba Proheebetit'.

'Keep-aff-the-grass' notice seen
in Dundee schemes.

Nuthinsup.

A no-score draw.

Wan-nuthin' youse anes.

We're losing 1–0.

J'git hut?

Was that a foul?

Fancy a gemma heiders or keepie-uppie?

Want a game?

Twa's up an' the ba's bust.

We're up the creek without a paddle.

Sweengin' at a ninoffensive wee ba'.

Dundee description of golf.

He's hooked hiz drehve.

Poor shot.

Synchronehsed sweemin's no' a nathletic pursoot.

An Olympic sport? Achawa!

Rest ashaired, exercehse nearly killed iz.

The gym's not for me.

Gie iz ur ba' back, ba'heid.

Hey, ugly, can we have our ball back?

KEN THIS

Complaints

F'ra the thanks Eh get.

I'm just not appreciated.

Sair fecht.

It's a hard life!

Eh'm pussay seek.

I'm a wee bit annoyed.

Eh'm as seek as a dug.

I'm fed up.

Eh'm a' Twi'urt oot.

I am bit tired of social media for now.

Twuzna me.

It wasn't my fault.

Expressions

Awa!

Really?

Eh, but Eh wull.

Yes, I will.

Na, but ye'll no'.

No, you won't.

Ma heid diznae butt'n up the back.

I'm not an idiot.

Ma heid's burstin'.

Too much information.

Dae Eh detect the Dundeh dehelect?

Parlez vous Dundonese?

Mind you wee buggers dinna be swearin'!

I don't want to hear of you youngsters swearing.

DOUBLE-YOAKIT

Yer at it!

You can't fool me, pal.

She yased tae be fairt o' spehders, but treh gettin' her aff the web noo.

Granny on Skype.

DOUBLE-YOAKIT

Wha bohked in the aspadeestra?

The leaves are looking a bit limp.

S'doonthi cundie.

Oh, dear, it's fallen down the drain.

Eh'm eaksy-peaksy.

Whatever...

Ho!

Excuse me.

'Kit 'at!

Look at that.

Jings, crivvens, help ma boab!

Well I never!

Beh'ir late thin niver, iy?

I'm here.

'EH HUD ME EHE ON A PEH'

Umma hearin' richt?

Could you repeat that, please?

Uv no' been daein' nothin'.

It wasn't me.

Um Eh speakin' tae m'sel?

I won't tell you again.

Hoo hud Eh no' thocht o' that?

Why didn't I come up with that?

'Sahfay.

Isn't that awful?

'Tsa wan tae me.

I am complete indifferent about it.

Geeza shot aff ye.

It's my turn.

Eh'm seek an' tired o' tellin' ye.

Don't you ever listen?

Ye'll get yer jotters.

You are risking your career with this.

Meh dowpee's awa' doon the cundie.

My cigarette end has fallen down the drain.

Eh've nae ehdea.

Sorry, I can't help you.

Dinna faff aboot.

Stop messing around.

Whutta flehg t'gie uz.

Goodness, you frightened me!

Gie hiz heid scalpers.

Give him a good No 1 cut.

It's a' goin' sweemin'ly.

Thanks, I'm well.

Gie it tilliz.

Give it to me, please.

Whit a sehze o' tohlay!

Does that excrement belong to you?

Eh'm yahnnin.

Excuse me for yawning.

Eh'm yahnninana.

Me, too.

Whut a turn t'gie onybody.

You could have killed me!

Izat the polis? Nah, it's me-maw.

Hmmm...

**Atween you an' Eh,
he's intehrely cockehed.**

Watch him!

DOUBLE-YOAKIT

Jist as hings were lookin' brah.

Not again!

Eh'll see whut Eh can dae.

Leave it with me.

DOUBLE-YOAKIT

I'ntit bogin?

Isn't it awful?

Hiz eggs are iywiz double-yoakit.

He's just a boasting blowbag.

DOUBLE-YOAKIT

She's upti hegh doh.

She's got herself worked up.